WHAT YOU SHOULD KNOW ABOUT THE CATECHISM OF THE CATHOLIC CHURCH

Charlene Altemose, MSC

LIGUORI
PUBLICATIONS

One Liguori Drive
Liguori, MO 63057-9999
(314) 464-2500

Imprimi Potest:
James Shea, C.SS.R.
Provincial, St. Louis Province
The Redemptorists

Imprimatur:
+ Edward J. O'Donnell, D.D.
Archdiocesan Administrator, Archdiocese of St. Louis

ISBN 0-89243-647-6
Library of Congress Catalog Card Number: 93-79929

Copyright © 1994, Charlene Altemose
Printed in the United States of America

Information concerning the specific contents of the *Catechism* has been taken from the Italian edition, *Catechismo Della Chiesa Cattolica*.

Cover design and interior art by Gary Currant

Contents

Acknowledgements and Special Thanks. 4

Introduction 5

Part I
    The Faith Handed on Throughout the Ages 9

Part II
    The Story of the *Catechism of the Catholic Church*. 21

Part III
    Basic Principles, Format, and Use of the *Catechism of
    the Catholic Church* 31

Part IV
    Contents of the *Catechism of the Catholic Church* 45

Appendix
    A *Catechism* Psalm of Praise 61

About the Author 63

Acknowledgments and Special Thanks

To Juli Peters DeLong, manager of information at the Catholic News Service, for providing valuable background information on the *Catechism* process by CNS news releases.

To Father Michael Camilli, MSC, assistant professor of historical studies at St. Mary's Seminary and University, Baltimore, Maryland, who so kindly shared his expertise and his volume of the *Catechism*.

To Father Michael Witczak, professor of liturgy and worship at St. Francis Seminary, Milwaukee, Wisconsin, author of "We Believe," a series of articles on the *Catechism*... and to the *Milwaukee Catholic Herald* for sharing them.

Most special thanks and appreciation to Kass Dotterweich, editor of this booklet, whose expertise, suggestions, and moral support have greatly aided in each step of the editorial process.

Introduction

  "We are drawn toward the Infinite; gladly we ride every wave which bears us toward it." That's how a poet describes the cravings of the human heart as it quests and searches to discover more about this world and the world of the spirit. Saint Augustine voiced these same sentiments: "You made us for yourself, O Lord, and our hearts are restless until they rest in you."

But we need not search hard to learn about God. Christianity is a religion in which God has revealed himself and shared his life and perfect love through Jesus. "Whoever loves me...my Father will love him, and we will come and make our dwelling with him" (John 14:23).

Jesus not only shows us the way to the Father but he "is with us always" (Matthew 28:20). Throughout two thousand years of Church history, we have had guideposts along the way, through which Jesus assures us "Yes, I am with you. Here is a gift of the Holy Spirit to guide you."

Catholics have been perennially graced with the gifts of the Spirit through the teachings of Jesus, the creeds, the sacraments, Scripture, sacred Tradition, the guidance of the magisterium, the writings and witness of saints and people of God.

The new *Catechism of the Catholic Church* comes as a timely gift to us for, in essence, the Lord is saying, "Here within these covers is the faith I ask of you at this moment; it is what you as Catholics have committed yourselves to at baptism. The *Catechism* is part of that legacy and comes as a special gift to you."

Vatican II opened the windows of renewal and allowed for diversity and flexibility in Church practices. Now that the Second Vatican Council is a part of life, we search for definite solutions to many timeless questions: "What are the changeless truths we uphold and what are the adaptations that can change?" "What does it mean to be Catholic today?" The *Catechism of the Catholic Church* gives us answers.

Laypersons involved in Church ministries are called upon to articulate and intelligently explain the truths of faith. No longer is the priest the sole "answer person" or "keeper of truths." Catholics today are challenged to renew and relearn the beautiful legacy we have in our two-thousand-year tradition. We are responsible for applying the ageless teachings of the Church to the modern world. The *Catechism* is here; we have no excuse.

The success of the *Catechism* is not to be gauged on the number of copies sold. Its success depends on the degree to which Catholics become more convinced, committed, and conversant in their faith. How we believe, worship, live, play, and pray are not contained within covers of a book, separated from real life. Like the Scriptures, which are worthless without being lived, so, too, the *Catechism* is a dead volume if the words do not come alive and become incarnate in daily Catholic living.

What You Should Know About the CATECHISM OF THE CATHOLIC CHURCH is a valuable guide to the *Catechism of the Catholic Church*. It is a launch pad for in-depth study of the *Catechism* and an intelligent reading of it. This simplified synopsis provides practical helps for using the *Catechism* and whets one's appetite to delve into the text.

This booklet is a handy resource for those who teach religion and share their faith. It is an affordable investment for adults who want background information about the *Catechism,* but have neither the reason nor the budget to purchase a copy of the text itself.

To tell the story of the *Catechism* and to make the *Catechism* familiar to the ordinary layperson so it is a welcome supplement to one's faith are the primary goals of this work.

As the human quest for understanding goes on, we need tangibles to give us a sense of security and certainty. The *Catechism* is a reassurance of the Lord's presence with us. The *Catechism* blends the riches of sacred Tradition with the insights of Vatican II. Let us not take the *Catechism* for granted, but embrace it as part of our faith heritage and as

God's precious gift to us today. Let us accept the *Catechism* with gratitude and make this our prayer:

> "You have given us much, O Lord;
> give us one more thing—
>   a grateful heart."

Part I
The Faith Handed on Throughout the Ages

O ur personal experiences of how we first came to know about God are as unique as our fingerprints. Some of us first heard about God at our mother's knee or in church as preschoolers. Some of us learned truths of faith in catechism class or parochial school. Others found the Lord after much searching and seeking. Those of us who received formal religious education after Vatican II have been exposed to various methods, texts, and catechists. All of us are still searching.

Regardless of our personal recollections, our faith journeys are part of that larger story of the Catholic faith throughout time. The story of the Church in its two thousand years combines the human quest for God with Christ's revelation through the Scriptures and sacred Tradition. Like the boy Jesus, the Church has "grown in wisdom, age and grace" (Luke 2:52). Each age, with its particular insights into the mysteries of faith, has attempted to understand the unchanging truths and to practice the Faith meaningfully in its time. Many dedicated persons have courageously overcome perils and hardships to spread the Faith and keep it alive. The following panorama touches on some highlights of the Faith as it developed and was passed on through the centuries.

As you go through this overview, notice the ebb and flow of the Faith. Chaotic situations in history seem always to have led to a spurt of growth and development through the power of the Holy Spirit, bringing greater focus and strength. The Church is at once human and divine. Because the Spirit is the wisdom guiding the Church, the divine

Continuing the Mission of Jesus

element has always withstood the vanquishes brought
about by human foibles.

The first several hundred years after Christ have come
to be known as the Age of Apostolic Witness and Proclamation. From the time that Christ told the apostles, "Go
preach the gospel to all nations" (Matthew 28:19-20), the
legacy of Jesus has spread throughout the world in various
forms, always with convincing enthusiasm.

The teachings about Jesus' life followed a certain
pattern: he was the Messiah who lived, died for our sins,
and rose from the dead. This "kerygma," or proclamation,
became the core of the Christian message. (See Acts of the
Apostles 2:14-36.) Beginning in these early years,
preaching the Good News was the prime method of
catechizing. The gospels were an outgrowth of this early
Christian preaching and of the early Christians sharing
their faith experiences and memories of Jesus in
community.

As the contemporaries of Jesus and apostolic witnesses
collated and carried the Faith into diverse cultures and
peoples, the Church spread rapidly throughout the entire
Mediterranean region. Although other recollections were
written, the four gospels were accepted as the inspired
Word of God because they mirrored most closely the
apostles' experience of Jesus.

Saint Paul was primarily responsible for bringing the
Faith to the Gentiles and for proclaiming the Good News
to the Mediterranean world. He explained the Christian
message in his many letters to the churches he established,
and in time, these letters –called epistles– became part of
the New Testament.

By the end of the first century, written instructions for
Christians and those entering the Church had been
compiled. The Apostles' Creed, formed from apostolic
preaching, was a summary of the teachings, along with the
Scriptures, both Hebrew and Christian Testaments.

These writings were significant to the faith of Christians
as they were persecuted for their beliefs (A.D. 64-305).
Instead of destroying the Faith, in fact, the Church
flourished, mostly due to the courageous witness of the

martyrs. Theirs was a unique form of evangelization that attracted many to the Faith. Writers who defended the Faith through this period (called apologists) include: Justin, Irenaeus, and Ignatius of Antioch. Since Christians were persecuted in the Roman Empire, some fled to northern Africa and formed faith communities there. In the second century, a catechetical school that served as a model for the catechumenate was flourishing in Alexandria.

During these centuries, Christianity came to be accepted and defined. In 313, Constantine issued the Edict of Milan which gave religious tolerance to all religions. Because Christians were numerous, Emperor Theodosius made Christianity the official religion of the Roman Empire in 381.

A.D. 300-500

HERESIES

DOCTRINES

As churches were built, the practice of the Faith became formal and structured. Because persons entering the Church had little if any religious training, they went through a formative process, the Catechumenate, which included instructions in the Faith and in Christian living. There was no separate catechesis for children; they entered the Church along with their parents.

The writings of the Church Fathers—Ambrose, Gregory the Great, John Chrysostom, and others—explained the truths of the Church and thus helped spread and strengthen the faith of converts. Interpretations varied. In the process of handing on the truths of faith, distortions and heresies crept in, like our childhood game "whispering down the alley."

Ecumenical councils defended the believers against errors and explained the divine mysteries in human terms. The formulation of the Nicene Creed, for example, began at the Council of Nicaea in 325. It states the basic Christian beliefs, and is recited each Sunday and feast day in Roman Catholic liturgies and in other Christian churches. In 420, Saint Jerome translated the Bible into Latin, the "vulgar," or common language, of the people. This Vulgate became the official Bible of the Church. Pope Saint Leo the Great also wrote profusely about Christian doctrines.

Just as the Church was on the brink of disaster with the fall of Rome and barbaric invasions, the Holy Spirit supported and guided the Church in proclaiming truth. The great figure of this era was Saint Augustine (370-430) who left to posterity a wealth of writings. He compiled a synthesis of the truths of faith, *First Catechetical Instruction,* which became part of catechesis and remained so until the Middle Ages. He taught Christian morality in the framework of the virtues and the Ten Commandments, which is still the model used in the new *Catechism.* He also countered heresy by explaining the concept of original sin and the need for baptism. Catechisms derived from Augustine's teachings set the tone for Christianity for over a millennium. His *City of God* and *Confessions* are perennial classics.

Up until the fifth century, formation in the Faith was directed toward adults, especially those awaiting baptism. But when baptism was taught as necessary for salvation, infant baptism became the norm. So the catechumenate and adult formation declined.

Whenever barbarians were converted, entire clans came into the Church, with no individual instruction or preparation. The only requirements demanded of these converts were that they give up their pagan practices, believe in Jesus, and live a Christian life of virtue. Minimal knowledge required was the Creed, and parents provided the moral training for their children.

A.D. 500-1000

MISSIONARY EFFORTS

COMMITMENT

During the early Middle Ages the Church experienced great strides in evangelization. Saint Patrick converted Ireland by 450 and Saint Augustine of Canterbury introduced Christianity to England and Wales in 596. The Faith was carried to Germany in 750 by Saint Boniface and into Slavic countries and Russia by Saint Cyril and Saint Methodius around 890.

Pope Saint Gregory the Great (590-604) introduced liturgical reform and stability into church worship and blended religious instruction into the liturgy. He introduced the type of music that came to be known as Gregorian chant. Since Christianity focused on the person of Christ, Christian feasts were substituted for the pagan festivals.

Islam, founded in 632, presented a formidable foe to the Christians. The Moslem takeover of Christian territory was quelled by Charles Martel, who halted the Islamic entry into Spain in 732.

Celtic monks evangelized the mainland and helped unify the Christian communities of Europe. The monastery schools became powerful centers of spiritual life where the laity learned the rudiments of the Faith. The monks contributed to the preservation of the Scriptures and classics, copying them artistically and painstakingly.

Charlemagne, crowned Holy Roman Emperor in 800, aimed to christianize all of Europe and made great strides in education. Alcuin, Charlemagne's capable adviser, developed curricula that served as a basis for educational methods. Students of the palace school became headmasters of cathedral, or bishops', schools, which soon rivaled the monastery schools as centers of learning. This revival, called the Carolingian Renaissance, brightened European culture during this time.

For the ordinary layperson during this time, faith remained rudimentary, transmitted primarily in oral form. In the eighth century, knowing the Our Father and the Creed were the only requirements for baptism and religious formation. Pastoral treatises stressed *living* the Faith above *knowing* the Faith because commitment at this time was more crucial than knowledge.

This era is known as the late Middle Ages. It was an era marked by dissension, conflict, structure, and organization. Eastern Christianity, centered in Constantinople, developed differently—both theologically and culturally—from the Western Church of Rome. Due to political and ideological disputes, the Eastern Church broke away from Rome and formed the Orthodox Church in 1094. Later, some churches returned to Rome and recognized the pope as head. Today, these are the Catholics of the Eastern Rite. The Church of Rome became more structured, and the Fourth Lateran Council (1215) codified Church laws.

In order to win back the Holy Land from the Moslem Turks, the Church conducted crusades from 1096-1274. Although not accomplishing their aim, the crusades hastened economic and educational progress and stimulated explorations and interest in travel.

A.D. 1000-1500

SCHISM

POPULAR PIETY

REFORMATION

The Renaissance, with its revival of culture and the classics, provided a fresh impetus to learning and the arts. Within the Church, however, dissension and conflict affected the hierarchy. The pope, acquiescing to French influence, moved to Avignon (1309-1377). When the papacy was finally returned to Rome, several dissenting "popes" reigned at the same time. This period (1378-1417) is called the Western Schism.

Obviously, this chaos made it impossible for the laity to depend on guidance from Church leaders, so they found other outlets to express their religious sentiments and to uphold the Faith. Religion, though still a vibrant force in life, assumed variant forms.

Saints Francis of Assisi and Dominic introduced an alternative form of monasticism: the mendicant lifestyle. They earned their keep by begging and instructed the people in the Christian truths through street preaching and evangelical witness. Their witness was powerful. The piety of the laity thrived on these saintly examples because the symbols of liturgy and the Bible were not known by the common folk.

In this atmosphere, the cult of saints took a hold in Catholic spirituality. When Christians who led pious lives were believed to answer petitions after they had died, prayers to these holy persons continued. Mystics who had intense religious experiences described their visions in accounts that became sources of people's devotion and faith.

During these years, morality and right living were stressed over intellectual understanding of the Faith. The spiritual life of the ordinary layperson was a religion of the heart and senses. Visual aids, art, music, and poetry were used to educate the masses and make their faith meaningful. Popular piety kept the Christian spirit alive. The Christmas crèche, the Way of the Cross, the rosary, wayside shrines, and patron saints for every human need are products of the piety of this age.

The most popular devotional book of this age was *The Imitation of Christ* by Thomas à Kempis (1380-1471). Another author who greatly influenced religious thought was Dante Alighieri whose *Divine Comedy* graphically describes the afterlife in an imaginary journey through heaven, hell, and purgatory.

Art, too, became a medium of the Christian message during this time. Stained-glass windows depicting biblical scenes and stories of saints were the "Bible of the poor." Miracle plays, also called morality or mystery plays, dramatized sacred stories for those who had no exposure to formal religious education.

Feast days were developed to give the peasants respite from slave labor. Each month was marked with an important feast, giving the peasants a day of rest and festivity.

This era predated the pen-paper-book age, so memory was most important in learning. Influenced by the penchant for numbers of the Jewish *kabbalah* and the Arabs' numerology, Christians in the Middle Ages devised ways to remember the truths of faith. Since the number seven had a certain mystique, Christian truths were taught in multiples of seven: the sacraments, the gifts of the Holy Spirit, the petitions of the Our Father, the theological and cardinal virtues, the capital sins, and the corporal and the spiritual works of mercy.

Academic interests, spurred on by the Renaissance, gave rise to large universities in Paris, Bologna, Salerno, Oxford, and Cambridge. These centers for learning provided professional training in the fields of medicine, law, and theology. Peter Lombard's explanation of the Faith in *Sentences* was a popular theological text.

The blend of Christian faith with Greek philosophy and reason gave rise to a new form of theological inquiry: scholasticism. Saint Thomas Aquinas outlined the schema of Roman Catholic doctrines in *Summa Theologica*, a classic theological text in seminaries after the Council of Trent. What Augustine had wrought for the early Church, Thomas Aquinas did for the Church of the Middle Ages. At critical junctures of history, these two theological giants provided syntheses of the Faith in great classics.

The dawn of the Black Plague greatly influenced religious thinking and spirituality. With death all around, people were more aware of their mortality and became preoccupied with the afterlife and eternity. Because many

children were orphaned, their upbringing and religious training often fell to the baptismal sponsors, who became known as "godparents."

The invention of the printing press by Gutenberg in 1456 revolutionized evangelical efforts. When books became more common and available, the Faith entered a new era. Translations of the Bible and books multiplied; the age of literacy had begun. As the computer has revolutionized communications in our age, so the printing press affected life and religion in the Middle Ages.

Political and ecclesiastical turmoil of the Middle Ages led to disquiet among the masses. An Augustinian priest, Martin Luther (1517) spoke out against abuses rampant in the Church, little realizing that he would spark the greatest upset the Church had ever seen: the Protestant Reformation. Attempting to make religion meaningful for the people, Luther translated the Bible into German and used practical ways to explain his views. The reform begun by Luther led to strong Roman Catholic resistance.

The Catholic Church launched a Counter Reformation with the Council of Trent (1545-1563). It defended the Catholic faith against errors, turned its attention to the deposit of faith and basic truths, and shifted the attention of the faithful to the importance of doctrinal correctness. The Council ordered seminary training for priests and weekly catechetical instructions for both children and adults.

The *Roman Catechism,* issued in 1566, was the first catechism for the entire Church. It was compiled as a manual for priests and a basis for other catechisms. Noteworthy, too, are the catechisms of Saint Peter Canisius and Saint Robert Bellarmine.

In addition to catechetical efforts, the post-Trent era was marked by copious efforts to check the spread of heresy and preserve the doctrines of faith. The Confraternity of Christian Doctrine (CCD) was founded in 1571 by Pope Saint Pius v to provide formal religious education especially for the youth.

The Church also became involved in works of charity and education which eventually led to the founding of apostolic religious communities. Saint Ignatius of Loyola founded the Jesuits, who became known for their missionary zeal and scholarship. Saint Vincent de Paul founded religious communities for men and for women who were devoted to the works of mercy. Saint John Baptist de LaSalle, founder of the Christian Brothers for the education of youth, developed practical methods for teaching. Saint Angela Merici founded the Ursuline Sisters who devoted their energies to education.

With the advent of scientific history, which looked at human existence from a chronological perspective, Catholics learned the Bible in story form as Bible history, with no specific emphasis on memorizing or quoting exact texts.

In the eighteenth century, when school attendance became compulsory, religious education moved from the home into the classroom and became part of the overall curriculum. Regional catechetics continued with no uniform text or method. A revised universal catechism was proposed at the First Vatican Council in 1870, but the plan was not realized because the Council ended abruptly due to the Franco-Prussian War.

In the first four decades of the twentieth century, teaching methods and timetables used in secular subjects influenced catechesis. In 1910, when Pope Saint Pius X decreed that children receive Communion at an early age, religious education became focused on children's preparation for the sacraments. Confirmation, celebrated in early adolescence, marked one's "graduation" from formal religious classes. Because religious formation was child-oriented, adult education and formation virtually disappeared.

Waves of immigrants who came to America in the latter part of the nineteenth century greatly affected religious education. They knew only their native language and thus depended on the schools for their children's education and formal religious instructions. The Council of Baltimore in 1884 consolidated religious training for the diverse peoples through the *Baltimore Catechism*, which became the standard text for all Catholic children educated in the United States.

This same Council, influenced by the work of Saint

Elizabeth Seton, decreed "beside every Catholic church a Catholic school." The parochial school system became a stronghold for the religious education of Catholic children in the United States. While children attending Catholic schools received religious education as part of their daily curriculum, children in public schools attended CCD classes (Confraternity of Christian Doctrine) held after regular school hours in parishes.

The method of rote memorization was used to teach basic prayers, Catholic dogma, and Bible stories. By focusing on pious customs and the folk religion of the "old country," the home reinforced what was learned at school. Ethnic groups retained their family devotions and rituals: for example, the sacred supper on Christmas Eve, Saint Nicholas instead of Santa Claus, blessings of Easter food, celebrations of patron saints' feast days, and shrines in the home. The Church of the early twentieth century in the United States was primarily an immigrant Church.

As cultures intermingled, the Catholic Church in this country became more Americanized and less ethnic. Along with this openness came a secularization in which religion no longer affected one's whole life, but was seen as only a part of life.

By the middle of the twentieth century, there was a worldwide need for basic values to counteract the influences of modern living. Methods of religious education used a Christ-centered approach and incorporated modern psychological insights.

In 1962, the Second Vatican Council convened. Because the Holy Spirit had guided the Church through turmoils in the past, hopes were high that this Council would lead the Church toward an understanding of herself as relevant and meaningful in today's world. It did. Vatican II (1962-1965) was a most timely gift of the Holy Spirit to the Church.

Never before has any religious body undergone such radical change in so short a time as has the Catholic Church since Vatican II. At the outset of the Council, the Church's self-identity, liturgical renewal, laity involvement, and relations with other faiths were dominant concerns—and changes were made.

These changes affected Catholic life dramatically. Vatican II catechesis utilized liturgical and biblical findings to reshape the content of the Faith in forms more adapted to modern life. A plethora of religion texts adapted Vatican II insights, and religion became more experientially related to life. Catholics became more involved in their faith and in their Church.

The RCIA (Rite of Christian Initiation for Adults), the process by which new Catholics are admitted into the Church, focuses on adult-centered formation. In some places, influenced by the RCIA, there has been a move toward a lectionary-based catechesis, that is, religious education based on the Sunday Scripture readings and liturgical themes. As lay ministers have become involved in parish life, adult-education programs have sprung up; graduate programs in theology for laypersons are available in many Catholic colleges.

Since the Council, religious education of youth has refocused on the family. Vatican II explicitly called on parents to take responsibility as the prime religious educators of their children. To keep parents informed of changes in Catholic practices, and to serve as a vehicle of adult-faith formation, parents are required to attend sacramental preparation sessions before their children celebrate the sacraments for the first time.

1962-TODAY

RENEWAL

CHANGE

VATICAN II

As much as these changes and shifts have injected vitality into the Faith, they remain "mixed blessings" because they occurred more rapidly than they could be assimilated. The constant flow of Vatican II changes caused the basics of faith to be overshadowed, making it difficult to distinguish between practices that can change and unchanging doctrinal truths. Children receiving religious education after Vatican II often did not know the basic prayers and fundamental Catholic beliefs.

Catholics have become unsure where the Church stands regarding contemporary issues and concerns, which results in both confusion of facts and hunger for guidance. This need for instruction and hunger for guidance is filled by the *Catechism of the Catholic Church*. It puts the Faith into proper perspective and provides explicit direction to

Catholics in today's world—as a new century rapidly approaches.

For adults, the *Catechism* brings a greater appreciation of the rich legacy of faith and a realization of a need for continuing formation through enriching religious-education programs. For children, it brings a greater integration of essential truths into religious education in a way that supports young faith in a challenging world.

The *Catechism* Is a Celebration

Although the *Catechism* is primarily an intellectual affirmation of our Faith, its contents are life-giving only when applied to daily living. The *Catechism* is primarily a celebration of God's works and our faith response in love. It balances our doctrines and traditional values, making these relevant to Catholics on the brink of the twenty-first century.

Above all, the *Catechism* will be a potent enabler, assisting Catholics to intelligently live out their baptismal commitment in the Church.

Part II

The Story of the *Catechism of the Catholic Church*

I n the previous overview, we saw how the *Catechism* has come at a fortuitous time in the Church's history. We now explore the beginnings of the *Catechism of the Catholic Church*, the complex process entailed in its compilation, its intended function, and some interesting data.

Clarification of Terms

For many, the word *catechism* brings to mind images of religion classes of yesteryear when catechism answers were memorized and recited at a moment's notice. For others, *catechism* has little or no meaning whatsoever. With this in mind, an explanation of the original meaning of the word and what it means today will be helpful.

The word *catechism* comes from the Greek *katechein*, which means to "bounce back," or "re-echo." In ordinary usage, it means "oral instruction." Since the early days of the Church, the word *catechesis* or *catechism* referred to the instructions one received in preparation for baptism.

Since the invention of the printing press, when books became a common means of communication, *catechism* has come to mean "a written text that contains the basic teachings of belief." Over the years, there have been many catechisms, usually written in a question-and-answer format. The *Catechism* expresses the Faith with declarative statements collated in a single volume in accordance with changeless and sacred Tradition and embodying the spirit of Vatican II.

Note how many words in our Catholic "language" derive from the word *catechism*:

- catechetical (kat'i ket'i kel): adj., applying to religious instructions; a catechetical textbook
- catechetics (kat' ket' iks): n., the study of religious education methods
- catechist (kat'i kist): n., a teacher of religious truths
- catechize (kat'i kiz'): v., to instruct, especially in religion
- catechumen (kat'i kyoo'men): n., one under instruction in the faith
- catechumenate (kat'i kyoo'me not): n., the process of admitting new persons into the Church; the Rite of Christian Initiation of Adults (RCIA)

Origins of the *Catechism of the Catholic Church*

The story of the *Catechism of the Catholic Church* begins at the 1985 Extraordinary Synod of Bishops held to commemorate the twentieth anniversary of the close of Vatican II. Cardinal Bernard Law of Boston voiced the consensus of the bishops and formally requested a universal compendium of the truths of faith that all Catholics hold in common.

Major steps in the development of the *Catechism*

1985: *Catechism* formally proposed at the Extraordinary Synod
1986: Catechism Commission of twelve bishops established by the pope, with an editorial committee of seven bishops and experts to assist in writing
1989: Working draft of the *Catechism* sent to all bishops
1990: Twenty-four thousand suggestions evaluated and incorporated into a new draft
1990-1991: Work on nine more drafts continues
February 1992: Completion of French draft
June 25, 1992: *Catechism* (French) approved by the pope
October 11, 1992: *Catechism* is announced in an Apostolic Constitution titled *Fidei Depositum*
November 16, 1992: French edition released in France, Belgium, and Switzerland
December 7, 1992: Italian edition available
December 8, 1992: Formal promulgation and solemn celebration of the *Catechism of the Catholic Church*

Throughout 1992: Other approved editions of the *Catechism* completed in Spanish and German; official Latin edition translation process begins

Throughout 1993: Editions in other languages planned

Aim and Function of the *Catechism*

"Preach the gospel wherever you go, and if you must, even use WORDS." This saying of Saint Francis of Assisi aptly describes the basic purpose of the *Catechism*: to put into words all the truths of faith that Catholics believe and live by. As a tangible statement and expression of our beliefs in a single volume, the *Catechism* aids us to better know and understand the Christian mystery as it is presented in a complete and concise manner.

The Catechism *blends Vatican II insights with sacred Tradition.* "The breadth and profundity of Vatican II teachings necessitate a fresh and thorough reflection to highlight the Council's continuity with Tradition" is how Pope John Paul II describes the role the *Catechism* plays in the Church today. Since the Second Vatican Council was pastoral in tone and not primarily doctrinal (no new truths defined), the *Catechism* integrates the insights of Vatican II with the unchanging doctrinal tradition of the Church. It portrays the unity of our Christian truths, while making a distinction between divinely revealed truths and those set up by the Church.

The Catechism *serves as a norm and point of reference.* The *Catechism of the Catholic Church* is described as "...a valid and legitimate instrument for ecclesial communion and a sure norm for teaching the faith" (Apostolic Constitution, *Fidei Depositum,* October 11, 1992). The *Catechism*, addressed primarily to bishops and those responsible for catechesis, contains all the truths that Catholics have in common. It serves as a frame of reference by which all diocesan and regional catechisms will be measured. Thus, it guarantees a doctrinal unity and certainty while it takes into consideration local issues and problems posed by the modern world and new situations to which faith and the Church must respond.

Preach the gospel wherever you go, and if you must, even use WORDS. St. Francis of Assisi

23

The Catechism *presents the one Faith to many cultures.*
Although the text of the *Catechism* is identical for the whole world, local editions will adapt it to the customs, culture, and way of life of specific people. Although Christianity transcends all cultures, the basic truths of the Faith can be incarnated into each. The *Catechism* serves as a buffer between the Church Universal and the Church Local. It is "catholic" in the truest sense of the word, portraying the unity of the Church while respecting the diversity of peoples and cultures that comprise it.

The Catechism *is a valuable tool for evangelization.*
Although there has been an upsurge of interest in continuing spiritual formation and information since Vatican II, many Catholics are not convinced that they could use further formation and catechetical instructions. The *Catechism* is an effective tool that provides Catholics with the information they need to be conversant and committed to the Faith. Religious-education personnel need to make the *Catechism* accessible to all Catholics by explaining its contents through education and instruction programs. The *Catechism* answers the questions: "How can adults become more knowledgeable in the Faith?" "What are the basics we should teach our children?" "What resource can we use to help others know about the Faith?"

What the *Catechism* is...What the *Catechism* is not.
- A complete compendium...not a summary or selecte beliefs
- A point of reference...not a textbook
- Set forth in declarative statements...not a question-and-answer format
- Truths already known...not new doctrine
- An application of Vatican II insights...not a Vatican II catechism
- A book for adult use...not a child's text
- The result of worldwide collaboration...not an original Rome document
- A springboard for catechesis...not a method of teaching
- An application of truths to our modern age...not a change in basic principles
- A tool for evangelization...not a lightly read book

- A guide for bishops...not for classroom use
- A basis for preaching/teaching...not a collection of answers to specific problems
- The authoritative teaching of the magisterium...not a proposal open to critique
- A statement of truths held in common...not a proposal for regional applications
- A basis for local catechisms...not directed at local issues
- A celebration of God's works...not a book of rules and regulations
- One of many catechetical tools...not the sole method of catechesis
- One complete text...not one book of many volumes
- A statement of our unity in faith application...not a command for uniformity
- Positive and objective...not subjective and opinionated
- An application of moral absolutes...not a list of new sins
- Affirming and pastoral...not polemical or argumentative
- Accessible and usable...not a "museum" piece

Interesting Facts About the *Catechism*

This background information helps us appreciate the vast amount of organization and expertise that was required to produce this monumental work.

Title: The official English title of the *Catechism* is *Catechism of the Catholic Church.*

Catechism for the Whole Church: This is the second catechism in which the Faith is presented to the whole Church. The first was the *Roman Catechism* of the Council of Trent (1566).

Universality: The *Catechism* is truly universal. Written by members of the Church worldwide, the *Catechism* reflects the collegiality of the Church. None of it was written in Rome except some suggestions offered by Pope John Paul II. The compiling of the *Catechism* required extensive collaboration with input from the bishops of the whole world.

Challenge of language: Among the members of the commission who had the task of writing the *Catechism*, seven languages were spoken. At first, it was proposed that

LATIN

FRENCH

SPANISH

ENGLISH

ITALIAN

GERMAN ARABIC

BURMESE

CHINESE

CROATIAN

CZECH

FLEMISH

GREEK

JAPANESE

MALTESE

NORWEGIAN

POLISH

PORTUGUESE

the working language should be Latin, but that was impractical and time-consuming. The commission then tried to have simultaneous working sessions in the major languages: French, Spanish, and English. This, too, caused linguistic difficulties. Therefore, the preliminary work was done in various languages and synthesized later into a single French version by the linguistic-versatile bishop of Vienna, Bishop Christopher Schonborn.

French edition: Because French was the common working language of the commission members, the first approved edition appeared in French in 1992, followed by the Italian, Spanish, and German translations.

Latin edition: The Latin edition will be one of the last translations completed. The Latin version is the official, or "typical," edition of the *Catechism* by which all other translations are to be measured. Other translations are called "approved editions."

Translations: Because quality and precision in the translations are primary concerns, it was not feasible to have simultaneous translations in all languages, like other Vatican documents. But translations are underway so the *Catechism* can be accessible to people as soon as possible.

The sequence in which the various translations appear will follow the rhythm of the different languages. Some languages, by their very structure, are more difficult to translate precisely and accurately. It is of paramount importance that the words used in each translation of the *Catechism* are understood in all languages in the way they have been originally intended. For example, the meaning in the French edition must convey the same meaning in each language: a mammoth contemporary Tower of Babel challenge!

Other translations planned (in alphabetic order, not in order of publication) include: Arabic, Burmese, Chinese, Croatian, Czech, English, Flemish, Greek, Japanese, Maltese, Norwegian, Polish, Portuguese, Romanian, Russian, Slovak, Slovenian, Thai, and Vietnamese. There is also the possibility that the *Catechism* will be translated into Albanian and made available in Braille.

The Catalan translation of the *Catechism* was presented to Pope John Paul II during his June 1993 visit to Spain. Catalan, a derivative of Latin, is spoken in Catalonia, Valencia, and the Balearic Islands and is the official language of Andorra, a tiny Catholic nation nestled in the eastern Pyrenees bordering France and Spain.

English version: The one authorized English version with identical text will be used in countries where English is spoken and used in education. The only variations in the English edition will be variant spellings in the British and American editions. Besides language and spelling, however, many other factors had to be considered in preparing the English translation of the *Catechism.*

The USA English edition publishers: The publishing of the USA English version of the *Catechism of the Catholic Church* is coordinated by the United States Catholic Conference and is available from thirteen Catholic publishers. This is the first time so many publishers have cooperated in a venture of this magnitude.

Challenges of the English translation: One of the challenging problems the English translation presented regards the widespread use of English. English is the second largest language in the world, besides Mandarin Chinese. Of the one hundred seventy independent nations of the world, English is the official language of fifty countries and the second language and education-business language in thirty-seven other countries. More than half of the world's nations, eighty-seven countries, speak English. Consider the cultural variety! English has even been the language of Antarctica because most of the explorers and expedition teams have been British or American. Besides being the most widely spoken language, English is the most popular second language.

Consider, too, the unique flavor of the English language in each area where English is spoken. To offer an English catechism that communicates the same meaning to the various strains of English-speaking people, while retaining the identical context, proved as challenging—if not more so—than compiling the *Catechism.*

Is it any wonder that it was such a great feat to produce an English version of the *Catechism* which is equally understood by all peoples who use English?

English as a word-rich language: Consider another aspect that the translators of the English version had to wrestle with. English has a larger vocabulary than most other languages and is a synonym-rich language. Many different words can be used to express one idea in English, whereas in other languages one word expresses many ideas. The hairline shades of differences in meaning between English words are linguistic hurdles that at times are difficult to overcome. In other languages, meanings of various words are easily derived from the context.

Inclusive language: Inclusive language is the appropriate use of words that do not denote a specific sex in cases when speaking of both men and women. In recent years, some English words have become more gender-qualified in ordinary usage. For example, words such as *mankind* or *man,* while in the past referred to both sexes, today are considered masculine-oriented and thus not proper to use when referring to both sexes. This concern is not a problem for everyone. But it is becoming more common to use gender-neutral words, such as *humans, human beings,* and *humankind,* when referring to both men and women.

This concern regarding inclusive language was taken into consideration in the English transition of the *Catechism* as it was also considered in the revised *Lectionary* and liturgical readings.

Horizontal and vertical language: The inclusive language issue deals with "horizontal" inclusive language: those words that refer to human persons. However, "vertical" language, words that refer to God, remains unchanged. We call God, Father, Son, and Spirit, and it is proper to use the masculine pronoun and adjective "he" and "his." The Church is feminine, referred to as "she." When referring to "people of God," "Body of Christ," or "temple of the Holy Spirit," the neuter pronoun "it" is used.

References and resources: The resources cited in the *Catechism* include Scripture, the Eastern and Western

Church Fathers, liturgy, the magisterium, ecumenical councils, the Code of Canon Law and the lives and teachings of the saints. Vatican II and Pope John Paul II are cited extensively. These references, from the tradition of the Church, show the continuity of the flow of Faith through the ages.

The *Catechism of the Catholic Church* is the newest link in the two-thousand-year-old chain of evangelization efforts to bring Christ's message into the world. It comes at a time when a synthesis of the Faith is sorely needed in order to present both the truth of the Church and sacred Tradition to the world in the light of the Second Vatican Council. The *Catechism* is a spiritual gift to the post-Vatican II Church that will affect the future only to the degree that it is received and appreciated.

> *Preach the gospel wherever you go, and if you must, even use WORDS.*
>
> *St. Francis of Assisi*

Part III
Basic Principles, Format, and Use of the *Catechism of the Catholic Church*

In order to benefit from the *Catechism*, it is helpful to consider certain theological premises and external features. In this section, we answer the following questions: What must one remember before beginning to read the *Catechism*? What are the external features and format of the *Catechism*? How is the *Catechism* arranged? What are some practical ways the *Catechism* can be used in various situations?

An essential ingredient for meaningful human relationships and encounters involves understanding the other person's viewpoint. Knowing the mind-set of the other makes for more effective communication.

The same is true of the *Catechism*. It is written with underlying convictions about God and what he has revealed to us through the Church. These theological presuppositions are basic to our faith-view; all other beliefs and expressions of the Faith flow from these primary truths. When you read, study, and reflect on the *Catechism*, it is necessary to do so in the following theological premises.

God is the beginning and end of all faith and catechesis. Although we may define religion as the human quest for the Divine, all religion is rooted in the very being of God. God is Love poured out in creation, who invites us into a

Basic Theological Premises Underlying the Catechism

deep and intimate friendship. Our religion is based on God as the Origin and Source of all faith.

In the *Catechism*, God is portrayed as a loving Father who, in love, beckons us and deals with us in our failings. The *Catechism* celebrates the continuing works of God in the Church. It is the serene and positive tone of a loving parent telling his or her children how much they are loved.

God has revealed his nature as Trinitarian: Father, Son, and Holy Spirit. All that we do is "in the name of the Father, and of the Son, and of the Holy Spirit." As Creator and Father, God lovingly brings and sustains all in existence. Through Jesus, we are redeemed, and through him, we relate to God. The Holy Spirit sanctifies us through the Church. All truths in the *Catechism* recognize the trinitarian aspect of God either implicitly or explicitly.

God is Mystery. What we know and believe about God and what God has revealed are truths too great for us to comprehend totally. We are finite creatures, and much of our understanding of God remains shrouded in the realm of mystery. We must be content to live with this element of mystery and trust in God's Word to us.

We respond to God in faith. God takes the initiative and reaches out to us. We are drawn by God to know and love him. Our positive response to these divine promptings is what we call "faith." The human part of religion is our response to the divine Mystery. This interplay of God in our life and our response to God is a covenantal relationship exemplified throughout the Scriptures.

Because we have been graced with the gift of freedom, our relationship with God is influenced by our will and desire. We assent to faith by accepting God's revelation and by faithfully living our personal commitment within the community of believers. The *Catechism* does not authoritatively dictate our faith, but lovingly elicits a faith response from us.

Human words are limited. One of the main gifts God has bestowed on us humans is our ability to communicate and make known to others what is in our innermost being. The common vehicle we employ is communication through words and language. Human language, as versatile as it may be, however, is limited by nature of our creaturehood.

The divine transmission of faith is timebound and limited in the confines of human words—for the divine Mystery is far grander than human words can explain. When we express our faith in the frail vehicle of human language, it will always fall short of the reality it expresses.

When we consider this aspect of the human word, we cannot but admire and respect those who undertook the gargantuan task of putting into human words the whole of our faith in the *Catechism*. More especially, we need to recall the task it has been to translate it into many languages so that the *same* truths are being communicated to all peoples. The *Catechism*, as a gift of the Church from the Spirit, is the handiwork of many experts who have wrestled with the limits of language to bring us a catechism we can all understand.

The truths of faith are expressed in analogous theological language. We cannot explain "all of God." But let us consider the specific role that religious language has in our understanding of our faith.

Spiritual realities must be couched in human terms, but religious language can express a spiritual reality only in analogous terms. We never fully capture the reality, but can "see" it in relation to what is familiar.

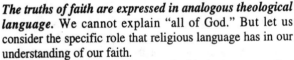

Throughout Church history, the challenge has been to put theology into human terms. At times, the language used imagery and symbols to capture the senses. At other times, the Church leaned on intellectual truths, as presented by the scholastics who borrowed ideas and concepts from the Greek philosophers. At different points in history, these explanations became one-sided or relied too heavily on one manner of explanation.

The *Catechism*, using rich scriptural imagery and intellectual philosophical rationale, attempts to present the Faith in a balanced view. There are truths that demand certain intellectual and philosophic explanations, and there are truths that are better understood when we "tug at the heartstrings" and allude to the senses. The *Catechism* offers this balance.

The magisterium interprets our faith. Some truths of faith are simply too immense to be grasped by our finite minds. Left to our own resources, the Faith cannot be grasped fully, for there is the danger of misinterpretation. The Lord has provided direction through the magisterium (the teaching authority of the Church), which interprets and explains our faith in terms we can grasp.

The *Catechism* reflects the magisterium at work in interpreting our faith. It comes at this juncture in history when we desperately need certitude and stability. The *Catechism* is one of the ways we come to know what is expected of us as Catholics. Unlike other writings, which are products of theological speculation and can be disregarded, the *Catechism* comes with the authority of the Church as the complete exposition of truths we hold as Catholics and that require our assent in faith.

All truths of faith are interconnected in an organic unity. Each truth of faith must be considered in relationship to the whole. The interconnectedness of all truths to each part is evident of the magnitude of the divine mysteries and the extent of God's love. Consider a lovely beaded necklace. Each bead is lovely, but not as lovely as the one stunning string of beads that constitutes the entire necklace. This bonding is clearly pointed out in the Apostolic Constitution that introduced the *Catechism*. The Christian beliefs in the Creed, celebrated in liturgy and sacrament, enable us to live the Christian moral life and to relate personally to God through prayer. Each truth is bonded with other truths and needs to be seen in the entirety of faith.

The *Catechism* provides a fitting forum for discovering a sense of cohesion within the truths of faith. No single aspect can be judged in isolation as a separate entity; it's always in relation to the whole Christian life. For example, the Church's stand on abortion flows directly from the Church's view on the sacredness of life and respect for life at all stages of development. The Church's laws and regulations make sense when they are seen in the light of underlying moral principles.

There is a hierarchy of truths of faith from which secondary truths have evolved. This is the basis of all our beliefs; each truth flows from this truth. The basics of belief are found in the creeds, and the basics of moral life are found in the commandments and beatitudes. Supplementary truths flow from these basic principles. The pope has likened the *Catechism* to a "symphony of faith"; the grandeur and beauty of a symphony lies in the overall unity of all instruments and all notes being put together in a grand unified performance.

So, too, with the *Catechism*. All the truths of faith are presented in a complete concise manner, but the core truths, and those more essential to the Faith, appear throughout the *Catechism*. However, the *Catechism* is so composed that one will recognize those truths that are basic and those that flow from the basics.

Our faith is ancient yet ever new. Thoreau once referred to a person's life as a river always traveling in the same channel, yet with new waters each moment. This also applies to the new *Catechism*.

Catholic doctrine is flowing in the same channel it has flowed for two thousand years, but each age has fresh insights and a different language to make it more understandable to a given age. The Faith of our present age is linked to the Faith of the past. Each age has built on the wisdom and insights of previous ages.

The *Catechism* is the Church's endeavor to amplify and sharpen the teachings of the Church in light of the insights of Vatican II. Nothing new has been added to the Church's doctrine in the *Catechism*. The "new" sins publicized by the media are not really new in the sense of never existing before. They are "new" in the sense that the *Catechism* points out specific behaviors of our modern age and the moral implications which flow from them.

As you read the *Catechism*, realize that old truths are seen in the light of Vatican II teachings, and that traditional truths are couched in new words. The *Catechism* is a gift to our age so we can better hand on the truths to future generations.

External Format and Features of the *Catechism*

The *Catechism* is basically a reference and catechetical tool. Like any other resource material, the effectiveness of the *Catechism* will depend on the creativity and ingenuity of those who implement its contents to serve their specific needs. This section provides a few practical suggestions about how the *Catechism* can be utilized in various ministries and parish programs.

Size and appearance: Whatever translation of the *Catechism* you use, whether hardback or paperback, the *Catechism* is a sizable volume: nearly six hundred pages. Although the outer appearance of the *Catechism* may vary from translation to translation and from publisher to publisher, the contents between the covers is identical.

Print size: As you leaf through the *Catechism*, you will notice various type sizes. The basic statements of the Faith appear in regular-size type. In smaller print, comments and quotations from various sources enrich and supplement the doctrinal material. About three thousand footnotes, found at the bottom of the pages, provide valuable supplemental information.

Reading level: Although the *Catechism* is addressed mainly to bishops, for their teaching mission, and to catechists, to be used as a tool for catechesis, it is compiled in language that the ordinary person can understand.

Catechism *logo:* Each edition will carry the official catechism logo: an ancient Christian symbol found on a tombstone in the catacombs of Saint Domitilla in Rome. It depicts a shepherd with staff and a flute in hand, sitting in the shadow of the tree of life with his sheep.

Of pagan origin, this symbol was used by the early Christians to symbolize the rest and eternal beatitude that awaits one who has faithfully lived the Christian life. The bucolic image also symbolizes Jesus as the Good Shepherd, who guides and protects his sheep with his staff.

With the sweet music of his flute, the Good Shepherd draws us to himself.

***Divisions of the* Catechism:** The *Catechism* is divided into four main sections called "Books." Each Book has two main Parts. Part One of each book serves as a general introduction for Part Two, which deals with more specific issues. For example, Book Four, Part One explains the nature of prayer and ways to pray; Part Two of Book Four, then, offers reflective meditations on the Lord's Prayer and the Our Father.

Parts One and Two of each Book are divided further into Chapters, which are subdivided into Articles, comprised of sections called Paragraphs. For easy reference, shifts in thought throughout the entire *Catechism* are numbered from 1-2865. Several editions may even include cross-references in the margin (as does the Italian translation).

References and quotations: Quotes and sayings from the rich treasury of Church traditions are woven into the main contents of the *Catechism*. These quotes and sayings embellish the text, provide valuable supplemental information and reflection, and corroborate the doctrinal material. The excerpts are marked by numbers after the quote and are identified in the reference index. The resources cited in the *Catechism* include Scripture, the Eastern and Western Church Fathers, liturgy, the magisterium, ecumenical councils, the Code of Canon Law, the documents of Vatican II, and the lives and teachings of the saints. Pope John Paul II is quoted one hundred forty-five times.

Sacred Scripture: Sacred Scripture is quoted directly or by citing the passage alluded to with "cf.," which means "compare with the direct scriptural text for a more thorough understanding." *The Revised Standard Version* (RSV) and *The New Revised Standard Version* (NRSV) are the editions of the Bible used in the *Catechism*.

"In Brief" sections: After each chapter or main section in the *Catechism*, an "In Brief" section summarizes the previous material and emphasizes important points of the section. These short, pithy statements make it easy to identify the core truths of the Faith. While these statements are syntheses of the main themes and linked to the doctrinal text, they cannot be considered in isolation without relating to the text. They are most useful as study helps and memorization aids in catechesis.

Indexes: Despite the vast amount of material in the *Catechism*, locating specific areas of interest is made easy with both an extensive Table of Contents and a thorough Index. The Reference Index has two parts: the scriptural references and the references from other Church documents and sources. The Thematic Index directs you to the passages dealing with specific topics.

Once one understands the theological premises and the basic format, the question remains, "How can we use the *Catechism* as a practical tool?"

Practical Ways to Use the *Catechism*

For general information: When you first glance through the *Catechism*, scan its layout and contents. Examine the Table of Contents to become familiar with the arrangement of topics. Get a general feel for the book and spot read certain sections, always keeping in mind to read the entire context. Although you might be interested in learning about a particular topic, always consider the topic in relationship to the whole faith. You miss the beauty of the forest if you focus only on a single tree.

Do not join a "catechism marathon" to see how often you can read the entire *Catechism*. It is more important to have the *Catechism* get through to you rather than you get through the *Catechism*. Pick up the *Catechism* itself and marvel at the splendor of God and the rich beauty of the Faith.

For a better understanding of specific Church teaching: Whenever a question of Catholic belief comes up in a casual conversation, or you want to know what the Church teaches on a specific matter, the *Catechism* is a handy reference. The subject of religion can often become a heated discussion in the workplace or during informal social gatherings. The *Catechism* provides adequate responses to any disputed issues. It states the teaching of the Church in a definite, concise manner. Rely on the Table of Contents and the Index to help you locate specific topics.

For enrichment and personal knowledge: Do not think for one moment that because you had eight years of Catholic schooling, you know all there is to know about the Catholic faith. You are enriched each time you delve into the riches of the Catholic tradition. You will marvel at how much there is to know about the Faith. A cursory reading of the *Catechism* will soon convince you of that. The *Catechism* is a rich reservoir of Catholic teachings, as well as classical writings. Even as I write this booklet, I am learning: new insights constantly surface.

For personal prayer and meditative reflections: The material in the *Catechism* is fruitful soil to nurture a deeper prayer life. By praying over the contents, and reflecting on the rich storehouse of resources quoted, one can come to a deeper understanding of the beauty of the Faith and the certitude it provides—not to mention the goodness of God. Especially helpful is Book Four, dealing with prayer; it explains the types and different ways to pray. Read each Article of the Creed and the Lord's Prayer in Book Four, and ask yourself what it means to you at this point in your journey of faith. Reflect on the deeper meanings of each phrase.

In ecumenical dialogue: As our global family shrinks, we are brought face to face with many different religions. Even in our personal lives, we constantly come in contact with people of other faiths.

One of the characteristics I have noticed in my meetings with people of other religions is the ease and openness with which they are able to discuss and explain their beliefs. This trait is not a common Catholic virtue, probably a carry-over from days when the laity depended on the clergy for explanations.

The *Catechism* can solve this dilemma and is a valuable vehicle for faith-sharing that provides certitude and accuracy. As an edicational tool the *Catechism* enables Catholics to discuss their faith in an intelligent, confident manner.

As a homiletic resource: For those who have the unenviable task of delivering homilies, the *Catechism* is an invaluable tool. It provides doctrinal corroboration of the liturgical themes and is a suitable means to educate the laity in aspects of the Faith. No longer will homilists need to wrestle with a proper interpretation; the *Catechism* provides certainty.

It is not sufficient, however, to preach on the *Catechism* in one homily and think one has done justice to it. The *Catechism* needs to be used as a point of reference in all preaching.

In catechist formation: While it is not essential that catechists have their own copy of the *Catechism* or read it from cover to cover before beginning to teach, those responsible for catechist formation are to introduce catechists to the *Catechism* so they can use it in their class preparations. Catechists should be familiar with the format and contents of the *Catechism* and have it at their disposal in the religious-education office or the parish resource center.

As a catechesis resource: RCIA team members and catechists will find the *Catechism* necessary in religious education and formation of new Catholics. The *Catechism* balances the life-experience aspect of the Catholic religion with an enriched intellectual grasp of the Faith. Although the *Catechism* is not designed to be used as a text in the classroom, teachers need to use the *Catechism* as a reference as they weave doctrine into their classes.

Catechists can fruitfully make use of the *Catechism* by considering the themes of the year and adjust their teaching from the *Catechism* according to the grade level. The national and local *Catechisms* will provide specific guidelines.

For theology students and seminarians: The study of theology holds a prominent, respectable place in the Catholic Church. Those pursuing theological studies and those training for specific ministries in the Church need to consider their sacred role in the light of faith and from the perspective of the teaching of the Church. Theologians research, interpret, study, and explain divine realities. But it must be done in the light of Scripture, sacred Tradition, and the magisterium of the Church.

The *Catechism* facilitates such theological studies and serves as the bedrock of all theological inquiry and speculation by articulating Catholic beliefs in undebatable terms. Theological conclusions must be in harmony with the doctrines of the Church as set down in the *Catechism*.

For parish and pastoral ministers: More and more laity today are called on to participate directly in the ministries in the Church. This not only requires a commitment of time and energy but also one needs to be formed and informed. It is important that lay ministers have access to the *Catechism* and be duly informed about its contents, especially those sections that deal directly with their ministry.

For parents: Vatican II explicitly declared that parents are responsible for the religious formation of their children. Although the Catholic school and CCD classes may take care of formal training, the parents are the backbone of children's religious and moral formation. Parents, as the "first church" the child comes to know, are bound to provide a suitable environment in which Christian virtues and Christian life can grow.

Parents can use the *Catechism* as a means to teach and discuss the Faith with their children. Imagine how fruitful it would be for the Church and our country if each Catholic family would use the *Catechism* on family-togetherness evenings for discussion and prayer. Parents and children together can discover and rediscover the legacy of faith as members of the great family of God.

In adult-education programs: Adults today are becoming more aware of their need to be knowledgeable in the Faith. More than ever before, they need to refine their childhood faith and come to a deeper understanding of what and why they believe.

The *Catechism* comes at a time when there is a hunger for unity and synthesis. Now is an appropriate time, a "teachable moment," when Catholics are more open to receive the direction and guidance the *Catechism* accords. The *Catechism* is a catalyst that can be the focus for a variety of adult-education endeavors.

With proper direction and motivation, those responsible for setting up parish programs can utilize the *Catechism* as the starting point and stimulus for their programs. A series titled "Becoming Catechism-Literate" or "Catechism Literacy for the Ordinary Catholic" can serve as a general introduction to the *Catechism*. Other courses could focus on each of the main Books of the *Catechism* or areas of specific interest.

Formally Introducing the *Catechism* to the Parish

The *Catechism* can be introduced meaningfully into a parish by a "Let's Welcome the *Catechism*" celebration. Such a prayer service demonstrates in a practical way the importance of the *Catechism* as a special gift of the Holy Spirit to the Church. (See the following page.) The success of the *Catechism* depends on how creatively and enthusiastically it is utilized in all areas of education and formation.

Prayer service to introduce the *Catechism*

Entrance procession and entrance hymn: While an appropriate hymn is sung, the pastor or parish representative carries the *Catechism* solemnly in procession and enthrones it in a prominent place set up in the sanctuary.

- *Opening prayer:* Thanksgiving for the gift of faith; petitions for guidance and direction in using the *Catechism*

- *Scripture readings* (such as Joshua 24:14-28, Isaiah 56:1-5, Acts of the Apostles 8:26-31, 1 Samuel 3:7-18, Galatians 3:23-29, 2 Timothy 1:6-14)

- *Responsorial psalm* (such as Psalm 1, Psalm 19:8-11, Psalm 25:4-15, Psalm 47)

- *Gospel readings* (such as Matthew 7:24-27, Luke 8:4-15, John 12:44-50, John 14:12-21)

- *Homily*
  1. The *Catechism*: a timely gift of the Spirit to the Church
  2. Excerpts from the Apostolic Constitution
  3. Background and rationale for the *Catechism*
  4. Definite practical ways the *Catechism* will be implemented in the parish

- *Intercessory prayers with response* (such as "Lord, we thank you for the gift of our faith.")

- *Formal presentation of the* Catechism *to the assembly:* Lift the *Catechism* high and present it to the faithful. The faithful respond by reciting the Creed.

- *Rite of Acceptance:* As a parish leader holds the *Catechism*, the people file up as for Communion. They make a personal assent of faith as they reverently touch the *Catechism* and quietly pray "Lord, I believe" or "Thank you, Lord, for the gift of faith."

- *Closing prayer, blessing, recessional hymn or instrumental*

Part IV
Contents of the *Catechism of the Catholic Church*

General Outline of the *Catechism*

Preface (1-25)

BOOK ONE:
The Profession of Faith (26-1065)

Part One: "I Believe"—"We Believe"
Part Two: Profession of Faith: Creeds

BOOK TWO:
Celebration of the Christian Life (1066-1690)

Part One: Sacramental Economy
Part Two: The Seven Sacraments

BOOK THREE:
Life in Christ (1691-2557)

Part One: Our Vocation, a Spiritual Life
Part Two: The Ten Commandments

BOOK FOUR:
Christian Prayer (2558-2865)

Part One: Prayer in the Christian Life
Part Two: The Our Father

Detailed Outline of the Catechism of the Catholic Church

The following is a detailed outline of the contents of the *Catechism* as translated from the Italian edition. Wording in the English translation may differ slightly. The numerical references, however, are identical in all translations.

This basic information, along with the *Catechism's* Table of Contents and Indexes, enables you to find those topics of concern that specifically interest you.

Apostolic Constitution "Deposit of Faith"
Preface
I.   The purpose of human life: to know and love God   1-3
II. Transmitting the faith: catechesis   4-10
III. The aim and intended audience of this *Catechism* 11-12
IV. The structure of the *Catechism* (four books)   13-17
V.   Practical instructions for use of this *Catechism* 18-22
VI. Need for adaptation   23-24
All done in love   25

BOOK ONE
The Profession of Faith

Part One: "I Believe"—"We Believe"   26

Chapter One: The Human Capacity for God
I.   The desire for God   27-30
II. Life leading to the knowledge of God   31-35
III. Knowing God through the Church   36-38
IV. How to speak of God?   39-43
In Brief   44-49

Chapter Two: God's Initiative and Encounter With Us   50
Article 1: The revelation of God
I.   God reveals himself in sign and goodness   51-53
II. The sources of revelation   54-64
III. Jesus Christ:
     Mediator and Fullness of all revelation   65-67
In Brief   68-73
Article 2: The transmission of divine revelation   74
I.   Apostolic Tradition   75-79
II. The relationship of Scripture and Tradition   80-83
III. Interpretation of the deposit of faith   84-95

In Brief   96-100
Article 3: Sacred Scripture
I.   Christ: The unique Word of Scripture   101-104
II. Inspiration and truth of the Scriptures   105-108
III. The Holy Spirit, Interpreter of Scripture   109-114
     The senses of Scripture   115-119
IV. The Canon of the Scriptures   120-127
     Unity of the Old and New Testaments   128-130
V.   Sacred Scripture in the life of the Church   131-133
In Brief   134-141

Chapter Three: Meeting of God and Man   142-143
Article 1: I believe
I.   The obedience to faith   144-149
II. "I know in whom I have believed"
     (2 Timothy 1:12)   150-152
III. The characteristics of faith   153-165
Article 2: We believe   166-167
I.   "Lord, look on the faith of your Church"   168-169
II. The language of faith   170-171
III. One faith alone   172-175
In Brief   176-184

Part Two: The Profession of Christian Faith
          The symbols of faith   185-197

Chapter One: I believe in God the Father   198
**Article 1: "I believe in God the Father almighty
              creator or heaven and earth"**
Paragraph 1: I believe in God   199
I.   "I believe in one God"   200-202
II. God reveals in his name   203-213
III. God, "Who is," is Truth and Love   214-221
IV. Consequences of faith in one God   222-227
In Brief   228-231
Paragraph 2: The Father
I.   "In the name of the Father, and of the Son
     and of the Holy Spirit"   232-237
II. The Revelation of God as Trinity   238-248
III. The Holy Trinity, a doctrine of faith   249-256
IV. The divine work and mission of the Trinity   257-260

In Brief   261-267
Paragraph 3: The Almighty   268-274
In Brief   275-278
Paragraph 4: The Creator   279-281
I.   Catechesis of creation   282-289
II. The creation—work of the Holy Trinity   290-292
III. "The world and state created
        for the glory of God"   292-294
IV. The mystery of creation   295-301
V.   God realizes his plan: divine Providence   302-314
In Brief   315-324
Paragraph 5: Of heaven and earth   325-327
I.   The angels   328-336
II. The visible world   337-349
In Brief   350-354
Paragraph 6: The human race   355
I.   "In the image of God"   356-361
II. "One in body and spirit"—
        Unity of spirit and body   362-368
III. "Male and female, he created them"   369-373
IV. The human person in Paradise   374-379
In Brief   380-384
Paragraph 7: The Fall   385
I.   "There where sin abounds,
        grace abounds even more"   386-390
II. The fall of the angels   391-395
III. Original sin   396-409
IV. "You have not abandoned him
        in the power of death"   410-412
In Brief   413-421

Chapter Two: I Believe in Jesus Christ, the Only
                Begotten Son of God
The Good News: God has sent us his Son   422-425
Jesus Christ: The center of all catechesis   426-429
**Article 2: "And in Jesus Christ,
        his only Son, our Lord"**
I.   Jesus   430-435
II. Christ   436-440
III. Only Son of God   441-445
IV. Lord   446-451

In Brief   452-455

**Article 3: "Jesus Christ, who was conceived
by the power of the Holy Spirit,
born of the Virgin Mary"**

Paragraph 1: The Son of God was made man

I. Why the Word was made flesh   456-460

II. The Incarnation   461-463

III. True God and true man   464-469

IV. How the Son of God is man   470-478

In Brief   479-483

Paragraph 2: "...conceived by the Holy Spirit,
born of the Virgin Mary"

I. Conceived by the Holy Spirit...   484-486

II. ...born of the Virgin Mary   487-507

In Brief   508-511

Paragraph 3: The Mystery of the life of Christ   512-513

I. The whole life of Christ is Mystery   514-521

II. The Mystery of the infancy
and the hidden life of Jesus   522-534

III. The Mystery of Christ's public life   535-560

In Brief   561-571

**Article 4: "Jesus Christ, suffered under
Pontius Pilate, was crucified,
died, and was buried"**   571-573

Paragraph 1: Jesus and Israel   574-576

I. Jesus and the Law   577-582

II. Jesus and the Temple   583-586

III. Jesus and the faith of Israel
in one God and Savior   587-591

In Brief   592-594

Paragraph 2: Jesus died on the cross

I. The trial of Jesus   595-598

II. The redemptive death of Christ
in the divine plan of salvation   599-605

III. Jesus offered himself to the Father
for our sins   606-618

In Brief   619-623

Paragraph 3: Jesus Christ was laid in the tomb   624-628

In Brief   629-630

**Article 5: "Jesus Christ descended into hell, the
third day he rose from the dead"**   631

Paragraph 1: Jesus descended into hell 632-635
In Brief 636-637
Paragraph 2: The third day he rose from the dead 638
I.   A historical and transcendent event 639-647
II. The Resurrection—work of the Holy Trinity 648-650
III. The meaning and power of the Resurrection 651-655
In Brief 656-658
Article 6: "Jesus ascended into heaven and sits
at the right hand of God the Father
almighty" 659-664
In Brief 665-667
Article 7: "He will come to judge the living
and the dead"
I.   He will return in glory 668-677
II. To judge the living and the dead 678-679
In Brief 680-682

Chapter Three: I Believe in the Holy Spirit 683-686
Article 8: "I believe in the Holy Spirit" 687-688
I.   The joint mission of the Son and the Spirit 689-690
II. The name and other names and the symbols
of the Holy Spirit 691-701
III. The Spirit and the Word of God
in the time of promise 702-716
IV. The Spirit of Christ in the fullness of time 717-730
V.   The Spirit of Christ at the end of time 731-741
In Brief 742-477
Article 9: "I believe in the
holy catholic Church" 748-750
Paragraph 1: The Church in the plan of God
I.   The names and the images of the Church 751-757
II. Origin, foundation, mission of the Church 758-769
III. The mystery of the Church 770-776
In Brief 777-780
Paragraph 2: The Church—People of God, Body
of Christ, Temple of the Holy Spirit
I.   The Church—People of God 781-786
II. The Church—Body of Christ 787-796
III. The Church—Temple of the Holy Spirit 797-801
In Brief 802-810
Paragraph 3: The Church is

one, holy, catholic, apostolic   811-812
I.   The Church is one   813-822
II.   The Church is holy   823-829
III. The Church is catholic   830-856
IV. The Church is apostolic   857-865
In Brief   866-870
Paragraph 4: The faithful—
     hierarchy, laity, consecrated life   871-873
I.   Hierarchical constitution of the Church   874-896
II.   The faithful laity   897-913
III. The consecrated life   914-933
In Brief   934-945
Paragraph 5: The communion of saints   946-948
I.   The communion of spiritual goods   949-953
II.   The communion of the Church
     in heaven and on earth   954-959
In Brief   960-962
Paragraph 6: Mary—Mother of Christ,
     Mother of the Church   963
I.   The motherhood of Mary
     in relation to the Church   964-970
II.   The cult of the Holy Virgin   971
III. Mary–Eschatological image of the Church   972
In Brief   973-975
Article 10: "I believe in the forgiveness of sins"   976
I.   One Baptism for the forgiveness of sins   977-980
II.   The power of the keys   981-983
In Brief   984-987
**Article 11: "I believe in the
     resurrection of the body"**   988-991
I.   The Resurrection of Christ and ours   992-1004
II.   To die in Christ Jesus   1005-1014
In Brief   1015-1019
Article 12: "I believe in life everlasting"   1020
I.   The particular judgment   1021-1022
II.   Heaven   1023-1029
III. The final purification in Purgatory   1030-1032
IV. Hell   1033-1037
V.   The Final Judgment   1038-1041
VI. The hope of
     a new heaven and a new earth   1042-1050

In Brief   1051-1060

"Amen"   1061-1065

BOOK TWO
The Celebration of the Christian Mystery

Introductory Passage on the Liturgy   1066-1075

Part One: The Sacramental Economy   1076

Chapter One: The Paschal Mystery in the Time
              of the Church

Article 1: The Liturgy—work of the Holy Spirit
I.   The Father, Source and End of Liturgy   1077-1083
II. The work of Christ in the Liturgy   1084-1090
III. The Holy Spirit
     and the Church in the Liturgy   1091-1109
In Brief   1110-1112
Article 2: The paschal Mystery within the
          sacraments of the Church   1113
I.   The sacraments of Christ   1114-1116
II. The sacraments of the Church   1117-1121
III. The sacraments of faith   1122-1126
IV. The sacraments of salvation   1127-1129
V. The sacraments of eternal life   1130
In Brief   1131-1134

Chapter Two: The Celebration
            of the Paschal Mystery   1135
Article 1: To celebrate the liturgy of the Church
I.   Who celebrates?   1136-1144
II. How to celebrate?   1145-1162
III. When to celebrate?   1163-1178
IV. Where to celebrate?   1179-1186
In Brief   1187-1199
Article 2: Liturgical diversity (rites)
          and unity of the Mystery   1200-1206
In Brief   1207-1209

Part Two: "The Seven Sacraments
            of the Church"   1210-1211

Chapter One: The Sacraments
        of Christian Initiation   1212

Article 1: The sacrament of Baptism   1213

I.   How it came to be called this sacrament?   1214-1216

II. Baptism in the Economy of Salvation   1217-1228

III. How do we celebrate
     the sacrament of Baptism?   1229-1245

IV. Who is able to receive Baptism?   1246-1255

V. Who is able to baptize?   1256

VI. The necessity of Baptism   1257-1261

VII.The grace of Baptism   1262-1274

In Brief   1275-1284

Article 2: The sacrament of Confirmation   1285

I.   Confirmation in the Economy of Salvation   1286-1292

II. The signs and the rites of Confirmation   1293-1301

III. The effects of Confirmation   1302-1305

IV. Who can receive this sacrament?   1306-1311

V. The minister of Confirmation   1312-1314

In Brief   1315-1321

Article 3: The sacrament of the Eucharist   1322-1323

I.   Foundation and end of life of the Church   1324-1327

II. How do we call this sacrament?   1328-1332

III. The Eucharist in the economy of salvation   1333-1344

IV. The liturgical celebration of the Eucharist   1345-1355

V. The sacramental sacrifice:
     action of grace, memorial, presence   1356-1381

VI. The paschal banquet   1382-1401

VII.The Eucharist—"Pledge of future glory"   1402-1405

In Brief   1406-1419

Chapter Two: The Sacraments of Healing   1420-1421

**Article 4: The sacrament of Penance
         and of Reconciliation**   1422

I.   How do we call this sacrament?   1423-1424

II. Why a sacrament of reconciliation
     after Baptism?   1425-1426

III. The conversion of the baptized   1427-1429

IV. Interior penance   1430-1433

V. The many forms of penance
     in the Christian life   1434-1439

VI. The sacrament of Penance

and of Reconciliation	1440-1449
VII. The acts of the penitent	1450-1460
VIII. The minister of the sacrament	1461-1467
IX. The effects of this sacrament	1468-1470
X. Indulgences	1471-1479
XI. The celebration	
of the sacrament of Penance	1480-1484
In Brief	1485-1498

Article 5: The Anointing of the Sick   1499

I. Regarding the essentials	
in the Economy of Salvation	1500-1513
II. Who receives and who administers	
this sacrament?	1514-1516
III. How do we celebrate this sacrament?	1517-1519
IV. The effects of the celebration	
of this sacrament	1520-1523
V. Viaticum, the last sacrament of Christians	1524-1525
In Brief	1526-1532

Chapter Three: The Sacraments in the Service	
of Communion	1533-1535

Article 6: The sacrament of Orders   1536

I. Why the name of sacrament of Orders?	1537-1538
II. The sacrament of Orders	
in the Economy of Salvation	1539-1553
III. The three levels of the sacrament	
of Orders (bishop, priest, deacon)	1554-1571
IV. The celebration of this sacrament	1572-1574
V. Who can confer this sacrament?	1575-1576
VI. Who can receive this sacrament?	1577-1580
VII. The effects of the sacrament of Orders	1581-1589
In Brief	1590-1600

Article 7: The sacrament of Matrimony   1601

I. Matrimony in the plan of God	1602-1620
II. The celebration of Matrimony	1621-1624
III. Matrimonial consent	1625-1637
IV. The effects of the sacrament of Matrimony	1638-1642
V. The blessings and responsibilities	
of conjugal love	1643-1654
VI. The domestic Church	1655-1658
In Brief	1659-1666

Chapter Four: Other Liturgical Celebrations
Article 1: The sacramentals   1667-1676
In Brief   1677-1679
Article 2: Christian funerals   1680
I.   The final Easter of the Christian   1681-1683
II. The celebration of the funeral   1684-1690

BOOK THREE
Life in Christ

Introductory Passage   1691-1698

Part One: The Human Vocation: Life in the Spirit   1699

Chapter One: The Dignity of the Human Person   1700
Article 1: The human person
              in the image of God   1701-1709
In Brief   1710-1715
Article 2: Our vocation to beatitude
I.   The beatitudes   1716-1717
II. The desire for happiness   1718-1719
III. Christian blessedness   1720-1724
In Brief   1725-1729
Article 3: Human freedom   1730
I.   Freedom and responsibility   1731-1738
II. Human freedom in the economy
     of salvation   1739-1742
In Brief   1743-1748
Article 4: Morality of human actions   1749
I.   The sources of morality   1750-1754
II. Good actions and bad actions   1755-1756
In Brief   1757-1761
Article 5: The morality of the passions   1762
I.   The passions   1763-1766
II. Passions and moral life   1767-1770
In Brief   1771-1775
Article 6: The moral conscience   1776
I.   The judgment of conscience   1777-1782
II. The formation of conscience   1783-1785
III. To choose according to one's conscience 1786-1789
IV. Errors in judgment   1790-1794

In Brief 1795-1802
Article 7: The virtues 1803
I.   Human virtues 1804-1811
II. The theological virtues: faith, hope, love 1812-1829
III. The gifts and the fruits of the Holy Spirit 1830-1832
In Brief 1833-1845
Article 8: Sin
I.   Mercy and sin 1846-1848
II. The definition of sin 1849-1851
III. The diversity of sins 1852-1853
IV. The gravity of sin: mortal and venial sin 1854-1864
V.   The proliferation of sin 1865-1869
In Brief 1870-1876

Chapter Two: The Human Community 1877
Article 1: The person and society
I.   The communitarian character
     of the human vocation 1878-1885
II. Conversion and society 1886-1889
In Brief 1890-1896
Article 2: Participating in the life of society
I.   Authority 1897-1904
II. The common good 1905-1912
III. Responsibility and participation 1913-1917
In Brief 1918-1927
Article 3: Social justice 1928
I.   Respect of the human person 1929-1933
II. Equality and differences
     among human persons 1934-1938
III. Human solidarity 1939-1942
In Brief 1943-1948

Chapter Three: Salvation in God:
              the Law of Grace **1949**
Article 1: The moral law 1950-1953
I.   The natural moral law 1954-1960
II. The old Law 1961-1964
III. The new law or law of the gospel 1965-1974
In Brief 1975-1986
Article 2: Grace and justification
I.   Justification 1987-1995

II. Grace   1996-2005
III. The reward   2006-2011
IV. Christian holiness   2012-2016
In Brief   2017-2029
Article 3: The Church,
    Mother and Teacher   2030-2031
I. Moral life and the Magisterium
     of the Church   2032-2040
II. The precepts of the Church   2041-2043
III. Moral life and missionary witness   2044-2046
In Brief   2047-2051

Part Two: The Ten Commandments

Introductory Passage   2052-2074
In Brief   2075-2082

Chapter One: "You Shall Love the Lord, Your God,
     With All Your Heart, Soul, Strength..."
     (Deuteronomy 6:5)   2083
Article 1: The first commandment
I. "Adore the Lord, your God,
     and him you shall serve"   2084-2094
II. "You shall adore only the Lord your God"   2095-2109
III. "You shall not have other gods before me"   2110-2128
IV. "Do not carve any idols..."   2129-2132
In Brief   2133-2141
Article 2: The second commandment
I. The name of the Lord is holy   2142-2149
II. The name of God pronounced in vain   2150-2155
III. The Christian name   2156-2159
In Brief   2160-2167
Article 3: The third commandment
I. The sabbath day   2168-2173
II. The Lord's day   2174-2188
In Brief   2189-2195

Chapter Two: "You Shall Love Your Neighbor
     as Yourself"   2196
Article 4: The fourth commandment   2197-2200
I. The family in the plan of God   2201-2206

II.   The family and society   2207-2213
III. Responsibilities of members of the family   2214-2231
IV.   The family and the kingdom   2232-2233
V.   Authority in civil society   2234-2246
In Brief   2247-2257
Article 5: The fifth commandment   2258
I.   Respect for human life   2259-2283
II.   Respect for the dignity of persons   2284-2301
III. In defense of peace   2302-2317
In Brief   2318-2330
Article 6: The sixth commandment
I.   "Male and female he created them..."   2331-2336
II.   The vocation to chastity   2337-2359
III. The love between spouses   2360-2379
IV.   Offenses against the
      dignity of matrimony   2380-2391
In Brief   2392-2400
Article 7: The seventh commandment   2401
I.   Universal use and private ownership
      of goods   2402-2406
II.   Respect of persons and their goods   2407-2418
III. The social doctrine of the Church   2419-2425
IV.   Economic activity and social justice   2426-2436
V.   Justice and solidarity among the nations   2437-2442
VI.   Love for the poor   2443-2449
In Brief   2450-2463
Article 8: The eighth commandment
I.   To live in truth   2465-2470
II.   "To render testimony in truth"   2471-2474
III. Offenses against truth   2475-2487
IV.   Respect for truth   2488-2492
V.   Use of the social means of communication   2493-2499
VI.   Truth, beauty, and sacred art   2500-2503
In Brief   2504-2513
Article 9: The ninth commandment   2514-2516
I.   The purification of the heart   2517-2519
II.   The struggle for purity   2520-2527
In Brief   2528-2533
Article 10: The tenth commandment   2534
I.   Inordinate desires   2535-2540
II.   The desires of the Spirit   2541-2543

III. Poverty of the heart	2544-2547
IV. "I long to see God"	2548-2550
In Brief	2551-2557

BOOK IV
Christian Prayer

Part One: Prayer in the Life of a Christian	2558
What is prayer?	2559-2565
Chapter One: The Revelation of Prayer	
The universal call to prayer	2566-2567
Article 1: In the Old Testament	2568-2589
In Brief	2590-2597
Article 2: In the fullness of time	2598-2619
In Brief	2620-2622
Article 3: In the time of the Church	2623-2625
I. Blessing and adoration	2626-2628
II. The prayer of petition	2629-2633
III. Intercessory prayer	2634-2636
IV. The prayer of thankfulness	2637-2638
V. The prayer of praise	2639-2643
In Brief	2644-2649
Chapter Two: The Tradition of Prayer	2650-2651
Article 1: The sources of prayer	2652-2660
In Brief	2661-2662
Article 2: The ways of prayer	2663-2679
In Brief	2680-2682
Article 3: Guide for prayer	2683-2691
In Brief	2692-2696
Chapter Three: The Life of Prayer	2697-2699
Article 1: The expressions of prayer	
I. Vocal prayer	2700-2704
II. Meditation	2705-2708
III. Oration	2709-2719
In Brief	2720-2724
Article 2: Difficulties in prayer	2725
I. The obstacles to prayer	2726-2728

II. Humble vigilance of the heart 2729-2733
III. Filial confidence 2734-2741
IV. To persevere in love 2742-2745
V. Prayer of the Hour of Jesus 2746-2751
In Brief 2752-2758

Part Two: The Lord's Prayer: The Our Father

Introductory Passage 2759-2760

Article 1: "The synthesis of the whole Gospel" 2761
I. The center of sacred Scripture 2762-2764
II. "The Lord's Prayer" 2765-2766
III. The prayer of the Church 2767-2772
In Brief 2773-2776
Article 2: "Our Father, who art in heaven"
I. "To dare to draw close
in full confidence" 2777-2778
II. "Father!" 2779-2785
III. "Our Father" 2786-2793
IV. "Who art in heaven" 2794-2796
In Brief 2797-2802
Article 3: The seven petitions 2803-2806
I. Hallowed be thy Name 2807-2815
II. Thy Kingdom come 2816-2821
III. Thy Will be done on earth as it is in heaven 2822-2827
IV. Give us this day our daily bread 2828-2837
V. Forgive us our trespasses
as we forgive those
who trespass against us 2838-2845
VI. Lead us not into temptation 2846-2849
VII. Deliver us from Evil 2850-2854
The Final Doxology 2855
In Brief 2857-2865

A *Catechism* Psalm of Praise

O praise the Lord, you peoples, praise the Lord all the earth,
For his goodness and love reaches out.
The *Catechism:* gift of God to the Church today.

We praise you, Lord, we thank you;
We accept your teachings and joyfully embrace
Your Word and the faith of our fathers.

Praise the Lord Through the Creed!

We praise you, Lord, as Father and Creator.
We praise you, Lord, as Son and Redeemer.
We praise you, Lord, as Spirit and Sanctifier.
We praise you, Lord, through your truth and your Church.
We praise you, Lord, through our beliefs and Tradition.

Praise the Lord in the Sacraments!

We praise you, Lord, through our baptismal commitment.
We praise you, Lord, in your Spirit's confirming strength.
We praise you, Lord, in your eucharistic presence.
We praise you, Lord, by your healing and forgiveness.
We praise you, Lord, through regeneration and new life.
We praise you, Lord, through our priests and ministries.

Praise the Lord in Living the Law and Commandments!

We praise you, Lord, for your love and laws.
We praise you, Lord, with your revered sacred name.
We praise you, Lord, through worship and sacred time.
We praise you, Lord, in family and authority.
We praise you, Lord, by reverence for all life.
We praise you, Lord, in truth and honesty.
We praise you, Lord, by respect for the earth's goods.
We praise you, Lord, by our love for all peoples.

Praise the Lord in Prayer!

We praise you, Lord, as we reach out to you in prayer.
We praise you, Lord, as we pray as Jesus did.
We praise you, Lord, as we honor your sacred name.
We praise you, Lord, as we forgive and are forgiven.
We praise you, Lord, for all your gifts and graces.

We praise you, Lord,
    through the *Catechism of the Catholic Church!*

                  Amen.

About the Author

 Sister Charlene Altemose, MSC, is a Missionary Sister of the Most Sacred Heart (Reading, Pennsylvania) with degrees in education, theology, and journalism. Her ministries have included teaching college theology, writing newspaper columns and articles, directing parish adult education, and being active in interfaith activities and the Council of Churches.

Sister Charlene was awarded a Fulbright scholarship to India and a Christian Leadership grant to Israel. As a result of her scholarship excellence, she was invited to be a presenter at the 1993 Council for a Parliament of World Religions.

Author of *Why Do Catholics...?* (Brown-Roa) and *What You Should Know About the Mass* (Liguori), Sister Charlene also gives workshops, retreats, and in-service or adult education programs.

More books about the Catholic faith from Liguori...

What You Should Know About the Mass
by Charlene Altemose, MSC

The who, what, where, when, and why of the Mass. Everything you need to know to celebrate the liturgy with spirit, enthusiasm, and significance to daily living. *$2.95*
Also available... What You Should Know About the Mass on audio. Two tapes. $14.95

The Catechism of the Catholic Church
Libreria Editrice Vaticana
Co-published by Liguori Publications

Part of the Church's official teaching. A positive, objective, and declarative exposition of Catholic doctrine. Hardcover English edition, *$29.95. Paperback English edition, $19.95. Spanish edition, (paperback only), $19.95*

A Catholic Guide to the Bible
by Oscar Lukefahr, C.M.

For each of the 73 biblical books, Father Lukefahr offers historical background, information about the biblical author, the literary style of the work, and a theological interpretation of selected passages. *$5.95*
Also available... A Catholic Guide to the Bible Workbook, $2.95

Handbook for Today's Catholic
Fully Indexed With the CATECHISM OF THE CATHOLIC CHURCH
a Redemptorist Pastoral Publication

A guide to Catholic basics. Includes applications of post-Vatican II Catholicism, integrating the Catholic faith into everyday life, and Scripture selections. *$1.95*
Spanish edition also available... **Manual Para el Catolico de Hoy,** *$1.95*

The Privilege of Being Catholic
by Oscar Lukefahr, C.M.

Explores how the Catholic sacramental view of the world is expressed in every aspect of Catholic life. *$5.95*
Also available... **The Privilege of Being Catholic Workbook.** *$2.95*

Order from your local bookstore or write to
Liguori Publications
Box 060, Liguori, MO 63057-9999
*(Please add $1 for postage and handling
for orders under $5; $1.50 for orders between $5
and $15; $2 for orders over $15.)*